The Writer's Room presents…

Topsy Turvy

The exuberant poetry of Vivien Neupauerova

Introduction by Paul Bellany

Afterword by Alice Bromell

info@creativewalden.co.uk

All rights reserved. No part of this publication may be reproduced, distributed, or transmitted in any form or by any means, including photocopying, recording, or other electronic or mechanical methods, without the prior written permission of the publisher, except in the case of brief quotations embodied in critical reviews and certain other non-commercial uses permitted by copyright law. For permission requests, write to the publisher, addressed "Attention: Permissions Coordinator," at the address above.

©2023 Vivien Neupauerova

Contents:

Introduction by Paul Bellany, Creative Walden 7

Hope   10

Lost in a book   11

Friend   13

Love   14

Me   15

Night   17

Dreams   18

In a hundred years' time   19

Broken Promise   20

Gymnastics   21

People   22

Mother Helen the Tortoise   23

Rainbow   24

My Alien Friend   25

Storm   27

Sun   29

The Oracle   30

Paul   30

All politicians should die   31

Sitting on my broom   32

Writer's Room   33

Book   34

Writer's Room   35

Easter   36

Alice   37

Afterword by Alice Bromell, Writer's Room   38

Introduction

She blew in with autumn winds, armed with a pen, an explosive wit and an enormous smile. Vivien Neupauerova had arrived, with a life force she could barely contain and achieving everything with a hop, skip and a giggle. Writer's Room would never be the same again.

Vivien had never written a poem in her life, yet here we are, less than a year later, publishing a book of her most accomplished work.

A voracious reader, Vivien devours books like a weightlifter imbibes calories, sometimes five novels in a week. It's even more impressive when you consider that these tomes aren't the comic-laden nonsense of David Walliams, so prominent on the children's shelves in WH Smiths, Vivien reads everything from The Hobbit to Michael Morpurgo to Jane Ayre and lots more in between. It's even more spectacular when you consider that Vivien achieved all of this while still only eight years old.

As well as writing the most fantastic poems, our latest Writer's Room author, composes ingenious hundred-word stories. I am always very honoured when I appear in these quick draw adventures, even if my character always seems to be fated to succumb to a gory but creative demise.

At the Writer's Room we believe in pure creativity. We don't focus on spelling or grammar, as the children seem to get little else from the English curriculum at school. We offer prompts, themes and ideas and stage regular group activities, but we also encourage attendees to write whatever they want and if they take all year working on a personal project then that's absolutely fine too.

We have a very diverse set of young writers, and every session is always very different from the last. No-one gets a sticker just for turning up, but those who have worked hard and shown their talent, as Vivien has here, have been published in the Writer's Room compendiums that proudly sit on the shelves of the local bookshop and Tourist information centre, as well as in the libraries of local schools.

The creative writing produced by children is no less important than that of adults. Eight-year-olds like Vivien have things to say that are just as poignant as seasoned authors. How many established storytellers can recite their works while standing on their heads? Well, our Vivien can and often does.

I count myself very lucky to be a custodian of such a fantastic group, and I know my fellow tutors Alice Bromell and Lee Dorrington do too. When the children turn their pens and pencils into wands and unleash their magic on the world, I'm delighted to be a front row spectator. More power to their elbows.

An enormous debt of gratitude must go to our sponsors, particularly the children themselves, some of whom have raised money by doing everything from selling cakes door-to-door to climbing England's highest mountain.

When you've finished this book, please pass it on to someone else so they can enjoy Vivien's uproarious take on life.

Paul Bellany

www.creativewalden.co.uk

July 2023

Hope

Hope is like a seed inside you

As it grows more blissful

But when it dies

It grows more doubtful

Hope is like a spark

It grows into a fire

Do not let it near water

Hope will retire

So never let hope die

It is your greatest possession

Rarer than gold

So never let it die, on any occasion

Lost in a book

A book is the key to my heart

Makes me feel ever so wonderful

While reading adventures

Makes me feel ever so hopeful

My heart tingles with joy

Fit to burst any moment

The bubble of happiness growing bigger

I feel enjoyment

I can't get my head out

It is too good

It might even

Change my mood

So, if you want me to listen

Never give me a book

I will read until I am an elderly woman

Always give me a book

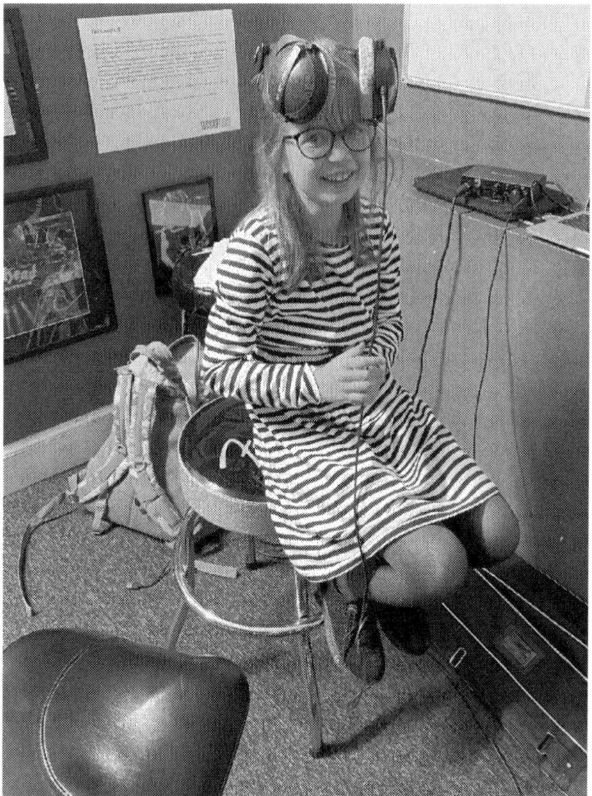

Friend

In my heart you will live

For ever and ever

And when I am feeling negative

You will comfort me

We will always cross the border of anger

Always and always

Because you are like my sister

Yes, like my sister

Sweet feeling, fill my soul

As always

Whenever I think of you at all

Always

You are my friend

Our friendship will have a sweet end

Love

The dew sparkles

Like glimmering marble

I always think of you

As I normally do

Lots of emotions wash over me

A glistening tear appears, I see

Your memories are branded in my brain

As clear as rain

Always remember you are my darling

Ruling over me like a king

Me

Introduction:

This is mine
That is mine
Mine
Mine
Mine
Mine

(repeat)

Verse 1:

This is my world
This is my life
This is my mind where thoughts wander
This is my home where my body lives in peace

Chorus:

This is my world
This is my life
This is my story
This is me and this is you
This is my universe

Verse 2:

You are my light
You are my life
You will guide me
You are my friend
You are my world
You are my guiding light

Chorus:

This is my world
This is my life
This is my story
This is me and this is you
This is my universe

This is me!

Night

The hedgehog wakes
It signals night is near
The owl hoots
It signals night is here

The sun
The darkness takes
The stars twinkle
The moon awakes

No more the piercing rays of sun
But the gentle glow of the moon
No more the loud, whispering wind
But the soft breeze that will roam

Dreams

I dream about sweets

On trees filled with treats

Dreams are wonderful things

They take you upon wings

And fly away

Upon the fairy rain

To a land filled with magic

Or any land of my pick

Far away, I look everywhere

From the tiniest ant to the biggest lair

In a hundred years' time

In a hundred years' time

Everywhere there will be crime

Human land balancing on trees

The temperature higher by a few degrees

The space underneath

For animals, beneath

Everywhere are flying cars

And there has been a discovery that aliens are on Mars

It is so wonderful

Where everything is colourful

Broken promise

One silent day a girl walked

To school

She talked

To her friend

And made her promise

Not to tell about the venomous

Snake she kept

Her friend lept

Over the fence

And asked for repentance

She gave it to her

Just to lure

Her best friend

Into keeping the vow

But suddenly she saw her friend telling about it

She was so tearful she had to sit

While her friend was devoured by the snake

And pills for her sadness she had to take

Gymnastics

Gymnastics is fun

As happy as the sun

It calms down anger

Inside any stranger

So, if you want to try it

On your bottom, don't sit

But on your hands

Wearing sparkly bands

Don't be lazy

Roll about and be crazy

People

One may be hopeful

Another sad

Another may be joyful

Another angry

One may be ugly

Another small

One may be pretty

Another tall

And they are all different

Faces, bodies, hair and personalities

And they have other enjoyments

Reading, learning, playing and watching

Mother Helen the Tortoise

One day, when walking down the road

An old woman who looked like a toad

Grey wiry hair hung over her face

Leaving a slimy glistening trace

"I'm a tortoise not a human," she complained

"You see, I have an invisible shell," she exclaimed

"Inside my shell are wonderful treasures,"

She said. "The computer has the most pleasures.

"Except that it keeps me alive

And helps me to thrive"

I run on immortal energy

As it is an ancient remedy

Please do not cut the cable

Otherwise, I will dissolve and disable

Rainbow

When colours form

After a great storm

It makes a rainbow

In your imagination it will show

A blissful moment in which

All feelings are very rich

An arc so big and wide

No-one from the rainbow shall hide

My Alien Friend

I am an astronaut, and I went to Mars

Where they have absolutely no cars

An alien sneaked on my rocket

And it pulled out a socket

Now me , Paul, is stuck on this planet

I'm thinking whodunit?

I see an alien

Who looks like a barbarian

He takes me to a science lab

And I think it is fab

Then the science person

Who, every second, his face seems to worsen.

I have to pose for pictures

And talk from scriptures

All these go to the newspaper

And I think the alien I found is a **traitor**

I plan revenge

Everywhere I scavenge

For a knife

To end a life

I finally found one

Phew, I'm done

The guilt in my eyes shows,

And to the betraying alien I go

I stab hard

Through the flesh and then I guard

For another alien who is as bizarre

Who rides on a star

Storm

Flashing lights appear
The dark clouds seem to leer

Frightening me out of my skin
Storms are not one of my kin

Props threateningly glaring
All the while they are dropping

Down below they splat
Everyone is frightened, even a rat

Then it seems funny
And the drops go runny

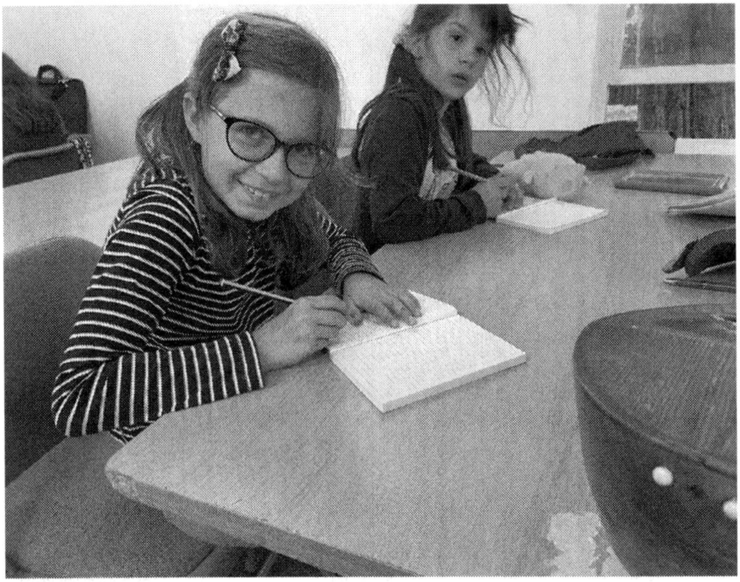

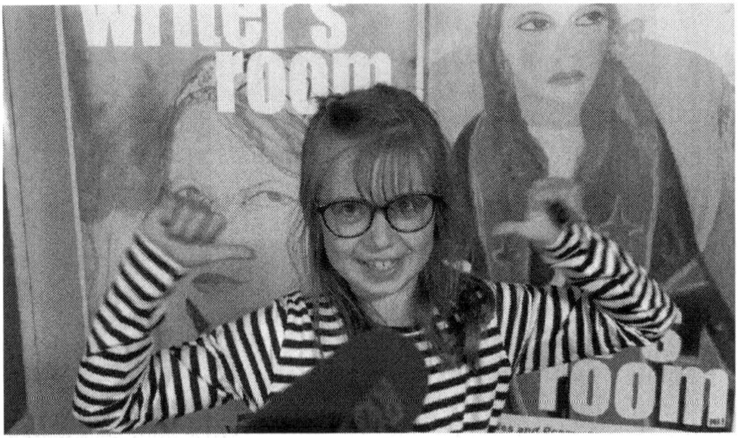
room
room

Sun

The sun is the hope in the sky
The signal for light way up high

Throwing rays of sun around
To planets which are found

The sun is like magic
And never grows sick

It is the beginning of our universe
Glowing sparks it will disperse

But further away
Maybe a gentle ray

Floats down
And wraps itself around the world like a gown

The Oracle

The power to see the future

To see if your life ends in manure

The Gods travel far to seek

The oracle, the opposite of the weak

When it dies another oracle will rise

By the end of a graceful sunrise

The other Oracle will stand firm

The spirit will learn to be an Oracle

Paul

Lots of wonder

So strong that there is thunder

I will bet for anything

For Paul an idea will ping

Or that he will throw himself

Even though he is smaller than an elf

Into the path of a mob that hates writing

And he will be the king

All politicians should die

Politicians should die

They all lie

An empty promise

False advice

Even if you think they are good

They are horrid

They trick you

So always with them argue

Sitting on my broom

"Hello, is this Writers Room?"
I called, sitting on my broom

Even though I am a witch
Of books, and a pitch:

I love Writers Room because
Of the way it soars

My soul and spirit
It would have a merit

And really it helps me
To become a lion or alien to be

Writer's Room

Paul is the head

But no-one listens to what he said

Lee is the assistant

But from writing he is resistant

Alice is the typer

And she is very hyper

They are all wonderful

And that makes Writer's room full

Paul is so funny

"Growl; says his tummy

So, before his tummy can complain

Writer's room is full of fame

Alice is beautiful

And Writer's room is wonderful

Lee is entertaining

And Writer's room is a king

Book

Tingles your heart

As refreshing as a tart

Every time you turn a page

Stories of excitement, sadness and rage

Transports you to a new world

Where hope is the ruling lord

A magical land

Anywhere, rock, grass or sand

And when time is up

You hold it like a cup

Full of special liquid

Savouring it, but the cup has no lid

Its enchantments spread everywhere

This magic is rare

It is called book

So come and look

Easter

The chicks get out of their eggs

And stretch their legs

The easter bunny is tired

Of all the egg rockets she has fired

But overall

It is all

A happy day

Beaming with sunlit rays

Chocolate everywhere

There and here

Alice

Alice is the best writer
She makes the world lighter

In Writers Room, she is the sun
And makes Writers Room fun

We are the planets
And she will always plan it

She shines and radiates
And always meditates

Alice is the best
She lives in a treasure chest

Afterword by Alice Bromell

It's hard to cast my memory back to Writers Room before Storm Vivien; there she was, an 8-year-old that declared herself to be a writer, despite having never before written a poem. One hour, several full notebook pages and at least five complete poems later, it was clear to see that she was, and is, in fact a writer. She continues to write a minimum of five poems every Wednesday evening, and each one carries the rare kind of artistic skill that most poets pour over a singular piece of writing for weeks.

In between her scurried writing, Vivien treats us to outbursts of the character behind the pen. This often includes handing out 'detentions' to me, Paul and Lee, usually for failing to satisfy a writing challenge she has set us, and always delivered to us with crossed arms, dramatic eye rolls, and a vivaciously drawn smile across her face. Since joining the Writer's Room, Vivien has turned up with jars of homemade writing prompts, initiated rhyming, drawing and handstand competitions amongst her fellow young writers, sang on stage, and recited in church. In fact, she recited a poem in Church that she had written just moments before, as I had managed to leave behind the piece of writing she had planned to read. Perhaps that time I did deserve a detention! Naturally, I was far more panicked by this than she was; Vivien simply tore off the back of the programme to use as paper, demanded a pen and then scribbled out a couple of lines on the spot. Ten minutes later she was at the front of the church reading into a microphone to an audience of strangers. Of course, she shot me many eye rolls throughout the service, which she had great pleasure in doing, and was both amusing and reassuring to me.

Whilst I hope my ability to be organised and prepared greatly improves, I do hope her ability to spontaneously whip up a masterpiece of words is never lost.

Vivien is the epitome of the reason we are so proud to run the Writer's Room. Without the space to come and write freely, who knows how many years it could have been before she discovered her statement to be true: a writer she is indeed, and a glorious one at that. She writes poems on her head and keeps Writers Room on its toes – here is to the marvellous mind of Vivien, her paper and her pen.

WALDEN Local

WRITER'S ROOM AT FAIRYCROFT HOUSE

Creative young writers celebrate their fifth anniversary with poetry, cake and pictures
(Photo: Martin Porter)
Story on page 4

Cake, pictures and poetry for Writer's Room fifth birthday

YOUNGSTERS FROM the Writer's Room at Fairycroft House, Saffron Walden, enjoyed cake, pictures and poetry when they gathered to celebrate the group's fifth birthday last week.

Since opening in 2017 Creative Walden have staged film and writing courses, shot a Zombie film that was premiered in a full house at Saffron Screen, performed an anti-drugs play for Essex County Council, run film make-up sessions, created music videos and dance projects and published three poetry books. An audioplay written by Writer's Room regular Alice Bromell was the subject of an interview for BBC Radio Essex last Tuesday when the power of creative writing to help tackle disorders and confidence issues in young people were discussed.

Said Creative Director of the community interest company Paul Bellamy: "There is still space in the older group should anyone wish to come along on Wednesdays at Fairycroft House.

"Give them the opportunity, the right guidance and commitment and young people can achieve anything."

Wednesday December 15 2021 **WALDEN LOCAL 9**

● Some of the contributors to the new Writer's Room book

Creative Walden publishes new book of poems and short stories

THE TOURIST Information centre opened its doors to a troupe of young writers last week for the launch of Creative Walden's new book of poems and short stories.

The Writer's Room Volume 2 features 42 poems, songs and stories from 22 local scribes aged from 8 to 22 years old.

Said tutor Paul Bellamy: "The variety of styles and content is astonishing and includes an ode to confidence from eight-year-old, Lily Frisenda Thomas, entitled 'I am powerful the way I am,' dynamic pieces from the Stabellini sisters, an enchanting Viking tale from Hattie Robinson, a great set of lyrics from accomplished musician Fynn Clement and seasonal poems from Lily Worboyes, Maemi Haining, Sam Parker and Daisy Burgess.

"Phoebe Kelly offers a poetic insight into sisterhood dedicated to her sister Anna who was unexpectedly taken ill recently.

"There is real depth in this collection. I'm particularly proud of writers like Alice Bromell and Izzy Logan who have shown great bravery in expressing their innermost feelings about great challenges they've faced in their young lives."

The Writer's Room group has been based at Fairycroft House since 2016, and runs two sessions every Wednesday night during term time.

Paul added, "All the writers worked very hard for the new book and earned their right to be included. I'm sure they will all receive a great boost knowing their work is on sale at the Tourist Information Centre and Hart's bookstore."

39

Performing with Lily Frisenda Thomas (Left) and Ellie Gill (Right)
for Ellie Grace and the Writer's Room, Winstanley LNS Fest, Christmas 2022

Information about The Writer's Room is available at:

www.creativewalden.co.uk

info@creativewalden.co.uk

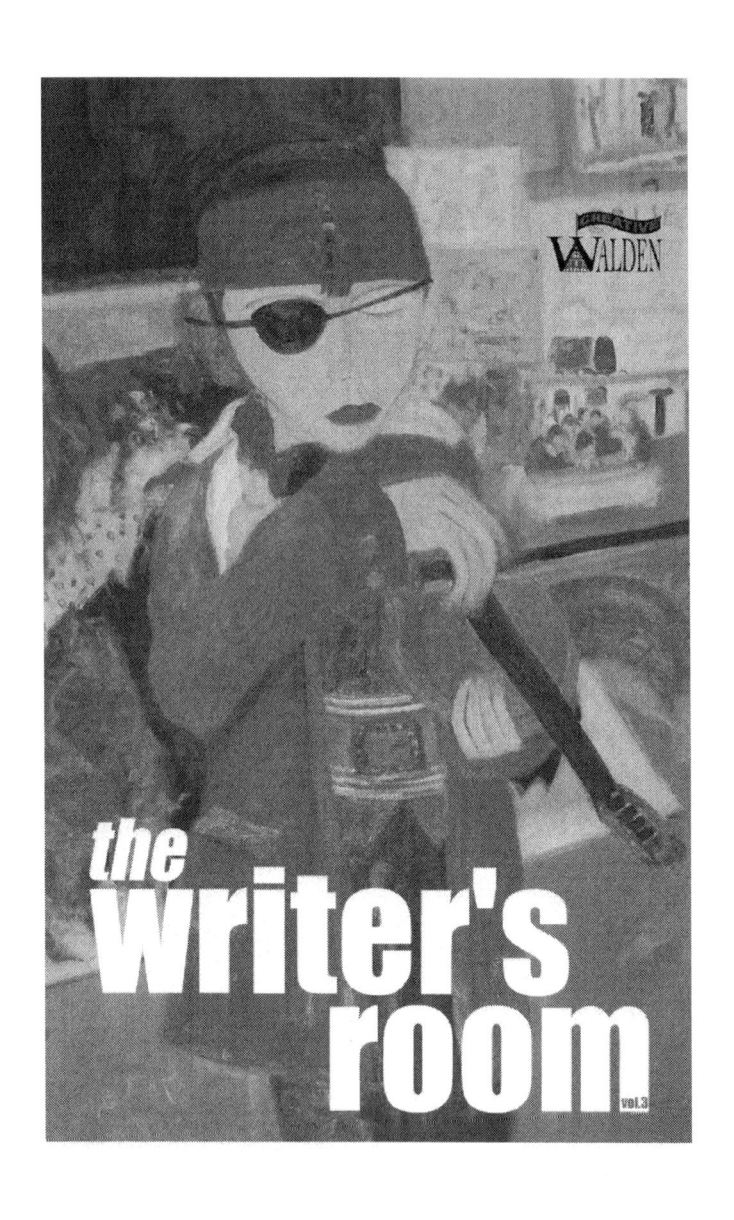

The Writer's Room volume 3 available Winter 2023

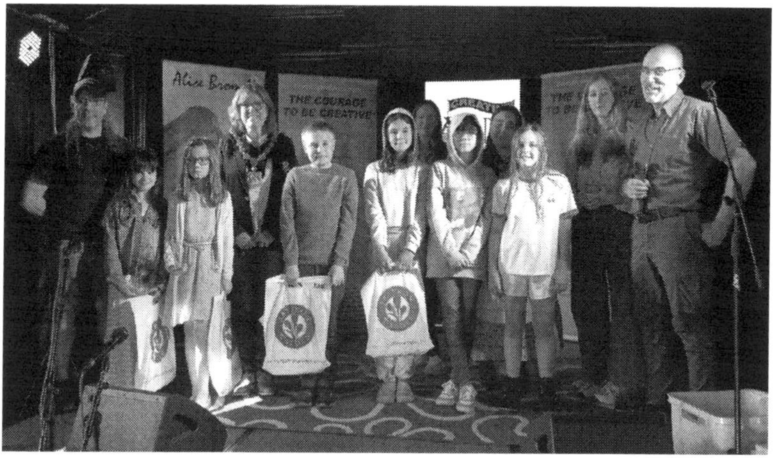
THE COURAGE
TO BE CREATIVE

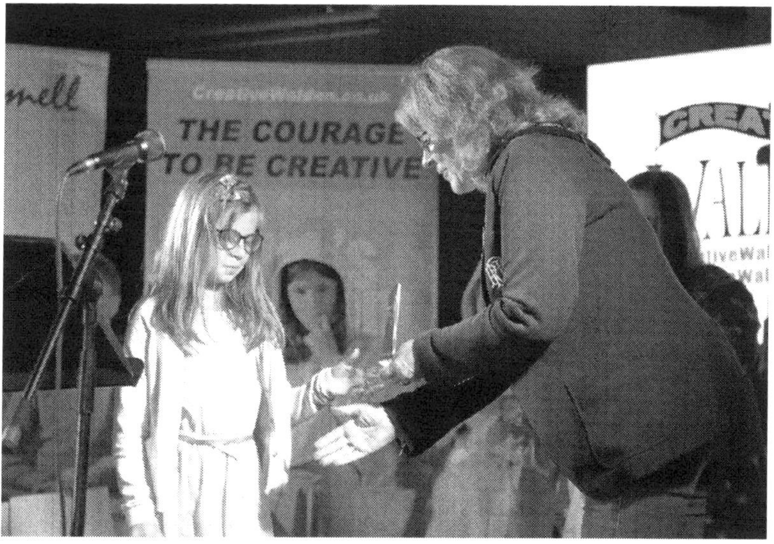
THE COURAGE
TO BE CREATIVE

Wednesday July 26 2023 **WALDEN LOCAL 3**

● Saffron Walden Mayor Heather Asker was a guest at Creative Walden's poetry recital on Sunday (Photo: Martin Porter)

Writer's Room perfect for nurturing creative talent

LITERARY STARS of tomorrow were on show at Creative Walden's poetry recital on Sunday when Saffron Walden Mayor Cllr Heather Asker handed out prizes, including Courage awards, to Lily Worboyes, 12, Vivien Neupaverova, 8 and Lily Frisenda Thomas, 9, who will all become authors in their own right this year.

Alice Bromell, who started six years ago as a young writer and now tutors the group, was awarded a special trophy for her poetry book 'The girl who decided to go for it'.

Said Paul Bellany, who runs the creative writing sessions at Fairycroft House: "There were many highlights of the evening including Izzy Logan's beautiful poem 'So long Sparrow' and 11-year-old Ellie Gill who brought the house down with her hilarious take on the trials and tribulations of travelling abroad in 'The 12 days of holiday.'

"We have children who have their own struggles in life and many on various spectrums but they all seem to score high on the happiness charts when they come to the Writer's Room and I thank them for sharing that happiness with Alice, Lee and myself. Wednesday nights are just the best"

One parent, Laura Worboyes, who, along with her daughter Lily, climbed Scafell Pike in May, raising over £2,000 for the group, paid tribute to Creative Walden: "Writer's Room has been amazing for us. It's the perfect environment for nurturing the creative talent of the young people who belong here. It's a safe, relaxed and fun environment that supports the writing and wellbeing of those who attend."

A film of the event made by Richard Bellany is available on Creative Walden's YouTube Channel.

Also available from The Writer's Room

On a Stream of Wonder

By Lily Frisenda Thomas

Available on Amazon and in audiobook format from Audible.

Printed in Great Britain
by Amazon